Origins

Meteorite Mission

Nick Ward ✶ **Jonatronix**

OXFORD
UNIVERSITY PRESS

Chapter 1 – The observatory

Everyone was excited. Miss Jones was taking the class on a school trip to High Tops Observatory. Ant could hardly wait. He loved anything to do with space.

"I've always wanted to go to an observatory," he said, smiling.

When they got to the observatory, it was getting dark. The coach stopped by a large building with a domed roof.

"They keep the telescope in the dome," Ant told Cat.

The chief astronomer was waiting to greet them.

"Welcome," she said. "My name is Professor Clark. I hope everyone is ready to do some stargazing!"

Chapter 2 – Through the telescope

Professor Clark led them into the building and through some double doors that opened with a quiet *swoosh*.

The children stepped into a large, domed room. "Cool!" said Tiger, staring in amazement.

Scientists were working at the computers all around the walls.

In the centre of the room an enormous
telescope was pointing up through a slit in the
roof towards the night sky.

"It's huge!" said Tiger. "How do you see
through it?"

"It's all done by computers," said Professor Clark. "We can turn the telescope to point at any part of the sky."

Professor Clark pressed some buttons and the telescope turned and tilted. A large planet came into view.

"Wow!" said Ant. "That's Saturn. Its rings are made of dust, rock and ice particles."

"Incredible!" said Max.

"There's more excitement to come," said Professor Clark. "This evening, you might even spot a new asteroid in the asteroid belt – one that scientists have never seen before. An asteroid is …"

"… a rock in outer space," continued Ant. "A large ring of asteroids orbits the sun, between Mars and Jupiter. That's called the asteroid belt."

Professor Clark smiled at Ant. "Well done!"

"Discovering a new asteroid is rare," Professor Clark added. "I like to wear my special necklace on such occasions. The pendant is made from a piece of meteorite. I'd be very upset if I ever lost it. Now, come over here and keep your eyes on the screens."

Chapter 3 – The missing necklace

The class watched the screens, spellbound. The telescope moved across a large cluster of stars.

"That's the Milky Way. It's all the stars and planets in the galaxy," said Professor Clark.

"There must be thousands of stars," said Cat.

"Up to four hundred billion!" said Professor Clark.

"How will we know if we see an asteroid?" asked Ant, as the telescope zoomed in closer.

"That's a good question," said Professor Clark. "Look for a moving dot amongst all the still ones. That will be an asteroid."

"OK!" said Ant, concentrating hard. Then – suddenly – Professor Clark let out a loud cry. "Oh no! My necklace has gone!"

Professor Clark crouched down to look on the floor. "I must find it …" she muttered to herself.

"Poor Professor Clark," said Ant. "She was standing by that table when she showed us her necklace. It might be over there. Let's go and look."

They looked all around, but there was no sign of the necklace. Then they spotted a metal grate screwed into the floor. Something was twinkling in the shadows under the grate.

"The necklace!" said Ant. "If we shrink, we can climb down and get it."

Chapter 4 – Rescue mission

Max, Cat, Ant and Tiger waited until no-one was looking. Then they turned the dials on their watches and …

They climbed through the grate and jumped down from one pipe to another. They soon found the necklace … but it was stuck behind a pipe.

"I've got an idea," said Ant. "If we can make a lever we can move the pipe slightly and pull the necklace out. Look! We can use this pencil for the lever."

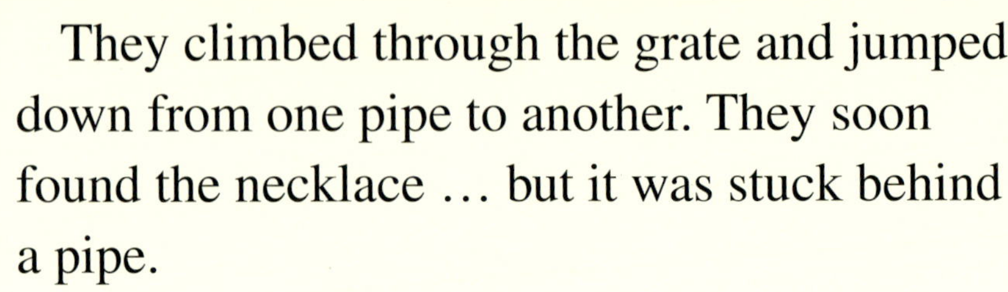

Cat and Tiger quickly carried the pencil over to the necklace.

"Now we need a fulcrum – something to put under the middle of the pencil so we can press down on it like a lever," said Ant.

"What about this?" asked Max, pointing to a large metal screw.

"Perfect," said Ant.

Max and Ant lifted the pencil, while Cat and Tiger rolled the screw beneath.

"Now all we have to do is push down on this end," said Ant.

The friends pushed down on the pencil with all their strength.

All of a sudden, the pipe moved a little and the necklace slipped to the floor.

"It worked!" cried Tiger.

"Let's hurry!" said Ant.

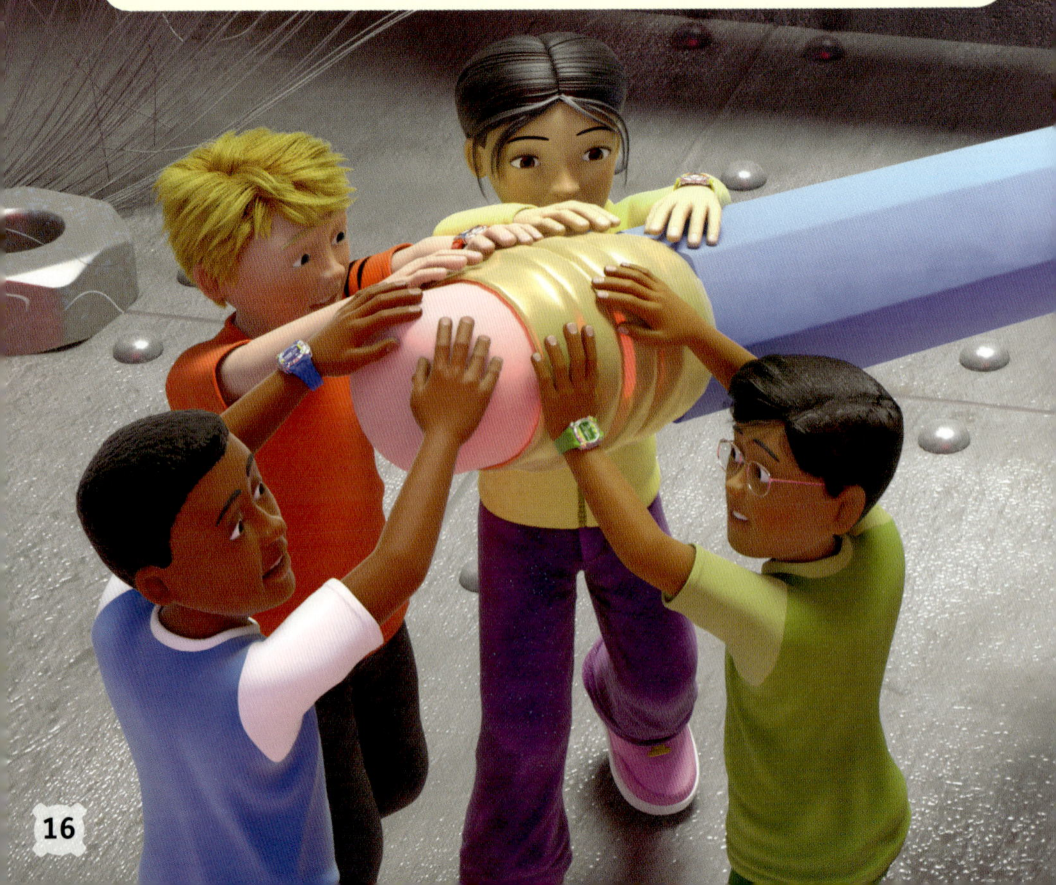

Max led the way as the four friends began climbing back up the pipes. Suddenly, everything went dark.

"What happened?" shouted Tiger.

"Someone must have covered the grate!" said Cat.

"It's really hard to see," said Max, trying to sound calm. "I can't see where the next …" It was too late. Max's foot slipped and he fell off the pipe!

"Help!" shouted Max.

"Tiger, can you use your torch?" shouted Cat.

"I think so," said Tiger. He held on tight to a pipe with his right hand and pressed the button against his head to turn on the torch. "Are you OK, Max?"

"I'm just hanging on," said Max, trying to swing his leg to the next pipe.

As Max spoke, light came flooding back in. "Phew!" said Tiger. "Come on, not too much further to go."

Chapter 5 – An exciting find

A few minutes later the four friends climbed out of the grate and grew back to normal size.

"I don't think I'll ever find my necklace," said Professor Clark sadly.

"Don't give up too soon!" said Ant, holding up the necklace.

Professor Clark turned around to face the four friends. A huge smile spread across her face as she saw the necklace in Ant's hand. "Wherever did you find it?" she exclaimed. "Thank you so much!"

"It was …" started Cat.

"Look, everyone!" cried Ant, excitedly pointing at a white dot moving on the computer screens.

"It's the new asteroid!" said Professor Clark.

Everybody in the room cheered.

"It seems you four are experts at finding things, old and new!" said Professor Clark, beaming with joy.